Slaying Retirement Risks

How to Create a Safe, Secure and Worry-free Retirement

MICHAEL MOE

Slaying Retirement Risks

Disclaimer

Although the author and publisher have made every effort to ensure that the information in this book was correct at press time, the author and publisher do not assume and hereby disclaim any liability to any party for any loss, damage, or disruption caused by errors or omissions, whether such errors or omissions result from negligence, accident, or any other cause.

ISBN-13: 978-1-946203-62-5

Contact Mike Moe.
Paramount Financial Resources
www.ParamountFinancialResources.com
MikeMoe@ParamountFinancialResources.com
Phone: 719-559-2544
Fax: 719-631-2576

Expert Press
www.ExpertPress.net

THE SOVEREIGN INTELLIGENCE ARCHITECTURE™

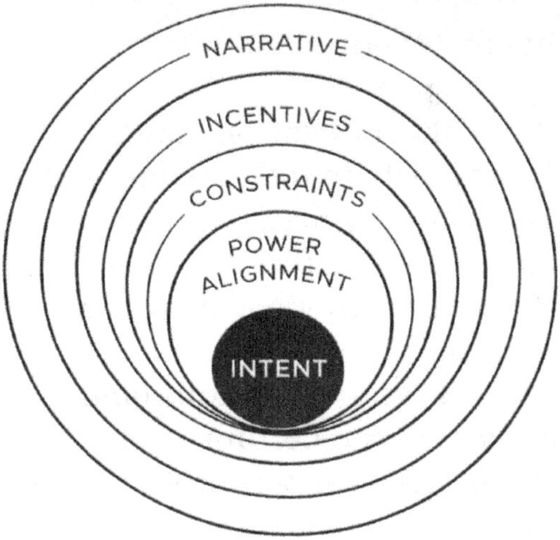

Conceptual refinement inspired by a converation with Dr. Joe Cozart, Jr.

ENGINEERED REALITY

The Architecture of Designed Environments

By Joe Cozart

Published by GMJoe™ Consulting.For inquiries, visit GMJoe.org

ISBN: 978-1-970547-21-4
Printed in the United States of America.

Table of Contents

INTRODUCTION

Dear Reader,

If you're reading my book about retirement planning, you'd probably think I was born an economic genius. Well, you'd be wrong. I was very good in math, but I didn't gain an understanding of finance until I was middle aged. But, please don't close this book—I have a story to tell that may benefit you.

Born and raised in California, I met my wife Becky in 1992 and we married in 1993. Soon afterwards, we made the decision to move to Colorado.

After a career in computer aided design and computer aided manufacturing (CADCAM) software, which included owning my own distribution business, I made an unexpected career change into the insurance business—a major career change at the age of 45.

Soon after I started, the insurance company I was representing transitioned into the securities business. In addition to knowing insurance products, I now had to offer my clients securities products. I remember thinking, "How am I going to survive this? I don't even know what a mutual fund is." I knew I had to learn, and learn fast, if I were going to grow my business and maintain my contract with my carrier. So, I studied and learned…and studied and learned…and studied and learned.

After all that studying, I realized the securities side of my business wasn't really my cup of tea, but I did love helping my clients develop safe, secure and worry-free retirements.

Since 2013, I've been, almost, totally focused on helping my clients develop safe, secure and worry-free retirements utilizing Fixed Indexed Annuities and helping my clients insure their retirement against market volatility and outliving their money. This has become my true passion. It's not even work for me. My client focus is on baby boomers and middle income earners.

As you'll find in this book, the answer to your retirement concerns can be found in guaranteed lifetime income and downside protection of your assets.

I'm what's known as a "safe money guy" in the industry. I work best one on one with clients. My goal is to share my knowledge with clients who have morphed from aggressive or moderate investors, into conservative investors due to market volatility and may be concerned about their financial future as they approach or are in retirement.

The reason I love working with these clients is because if I wasn't in this business, I would be living the life of one of my clients. Getting to know my clients is sometimes like looking into a mirror of what my life could have been not knowing, if I'd saved enough, how to protect what I'd saved, and most of all, outliving my money.

I'm a regular person—just like you. My wife is a piano teacher. We are not super wealthy people. But, we have been totally blessed with this knowledge. I could retire right now and be fine, but it is my mission—my calling—to share this knowledge with my clients.

Currently, my personal planned retirement position is excellent, but, only because of what I was forced to learn, starting in 1998, in order to advance my career.

Why am I telling you this? It's because hardly a day goes by that I don't think about the retirement position that I would be in if I hadn't entered this industry.

I have many colleagues in my business that are 15-35 years younger than I am who are very successful, and there are many things I continue to learn from them. But...the one thing they don't get is the emotional side of this business. When I sit down with a future client for the first time, I can see the concern in their eyes and I know exactly what they're thinking.

So, it is my honor to share this book with you and I hope you'll find it useful.

Happy Reading!

Mike Moe

P.S. I dedicate this book to my wife, Becky. Without her, I wouldn't be where I am today. I married her at 40, and it is the love I have for her that motivated me to be a better provider. This includes providing for the last third of our lives, also known as retirement. Becky and my two step daughters, Heather and Collette are the three loves of my life.

"...with God, all things are possible."

Matthew 19:26

Chapter 1

Our First Meeting: What to Expect

I believe that meeting a client face to face is critical because looking a person in the eyes is what creates the beginning of trust in our new relationship.

You see, when it comes to their financial future, many investors are experiencing extreme concern. Well, I guess you could say this is fairly common when it comes to my clients, because I only work with later life investors who are facing retirement in the next few years and are nearing, or have finished, the earning phase of their lives.

Quite often, their concern stems from the fact that they have a fear of "not having enough." What will retirement be like if I run out of money? How much money do I even need in the first place? Or, maybe, I've trusted before, and that trust was violated—why should I trust you?

I understand all these concerns, and frankly, I'd be in exactly your same position if I hadn't taken a major career detour into the finance world all those years ago.

I mean, until I learned this business, I was in the dark just like many of my clients. When the light came on for me, it changed my life. And, that's my life's goal, to turn on that same light for others.

Before I retire, I want to educate, advise, and offer support to as many clients as possible. And that's why I want to meet with you.

So, after we set up our appointment, I recommend holding the meetings in your home. The reason for this is two-fold. For one, I can get a good sense of the client just by visiting their home. That sense helps me understand their life and goals. And, secondly, it makes our meeting much more productive. For example, if I need particular paperwork (such as a financial statement, etc.) then they can conveniently retrieve it and we can keep the process flowing.

This method works so well for me versus them coming to an office. The office setting is much less personal and doesn't do a whole lot for establishing the client/advisor rapport that is so important.

What can you expect at this meeting?

We'll go through an in-depth questionnaire process. You'll find that my questions are deeper than just fact-based information or numbers. I like to provoke conversations. And, again, this will give me a better sense of the whole individual and what your needs and concerns might be.

Here are just a few examples of the questions I will ask:

"How would it make you feel if we could eliminate the unknown?"

"How would it impact you if there was a significant market downturn over a short period of time and you lost 30% of your retirement savings?"

"How does it make you feel when there's a significant drop in the market?"

Other than discussing just standard assets and liabilities, it is important to look at the full picture of your retirement.

"When do you plan on retiring?"

"Is the possibility of outliving your money a concern for you?"

"Are you confident your spouse would be provided for if he/she outlived you?"

"What type of work have you done?"

"What types of things are you looking forward to doing during your retirement?"

"What excites you about retirement?"

"What concerns you about retirement?"

After the meeting, I will generate a Retirement Income Report for you which will show you what your projected income will be from all your retirement sources at your target retirement date and going forward.

Chapter 2

Addressing Your Concerns

As retirement draws near, you may start to worry. Quite often, when people turn 50, that's when the retirement light starts to go on. "Holy cow, this retirement thing is really going to happen. I thought retirement was just for dinosaurs, but I'm growing scales." This is totally natural, trust me.

But, I must tell you that you are far from alone in your concerns. The good news is that I deal with this concern daily and I'm here to help you.

Sometimes when clients come to me, they have saved money for years, but they're concerned if it will be enough to support them for the full length of their retirement.

The truth is that they often don't have anywhere near the amount of money that they'll need to maintain their current lifestyle throughout retirement. Even with Social Security benefits added into the mix, it is just simply not enough.

If you are a baby boomer and have concerns about retirement, I can help.

Several years ago, I was marketing my business using a Social Security maximization advertising campaign. As it implies, I would show couples different strategies to maximize their Social Security income.

After completing dozens of these, I was stunned to discover how many people were financially unprepared for retirement. Many of them had few other options than to just keep working.

So, why is it that so many boomers are struggling with retirement income planning?

One of the biggest reasons is that the baby boomer generation didn't learn much about retirement planning from our parents. Oh sure, we heard "save money for a rainy day" plenty of times. But, not much, if anything, about actual retirement planning.

When I speak of "our parents" I'm referring to the generation ahead of baby boomers. Here's how they were different:

- Many of them working in the private sector had pension plans.
- They were far less transient and rarely moved.
- They paid off their mortgages when they were in their 50's.

Compare this to our generation:

- Pension plans in the private sector have diminished to the point of near non-existence over the past few decades.
- We are far more transient than our parents, moving frequently and starting new jobs, or being relocated often.

- Many of us begin new mortgages in our 50's, instead of paying them off.

So, with a paid off house, a monthly pension check to go along with two social security checks, what was there for our parents to teach us about retirement planning?

The result is that most middle income earners don't save enough. We are, in fact, still transitional from the pension plan era. And, many clients are misinformed when they are led to believe that a company sponsored retirement plan (401(k), 403(b), 457, etc.) is an adequate replacement for an old fashioned pension plan. These plans are savings plans, not income plans.

This has Americans approaching retirement left with inadequate savings for retirement. In fact, one-third of workers age 55 or older have a nest egg of less than $25,000. Does that sound like enough to provide for you and your spouse for the next 25 to 30 years? Many people don't think about the obvious. If $25,000 isn't nearly enough for one year of living expenses now, how much income should someone expect out of $25,000 through 25 years, or more, of retirement?

A recent Boston College study found that when kids leave home, empty-nesters typically increase their 401(k) saving by less than 1% of pay. If unemployment, market volatility, health issues, or college costs have taken a bite out of that nest egg, it may not be large enough to allow them to retire on schedule.

The "greatest generation" had a culture of saving. Its thrift was reinforced further by hard times and a call for personal sacrifices as the economy endured the great depression and stateside rationing during WWII. The commerce department began measuring household savings in 1959, and as unbelievable as it may seem today, households saved 10% or more of their disposable incomes through nearly all of the sixties.

More spending means less saving, and Americans are plagued by insufficient retirement reserves. For many, retirement may not even be on the radar. Some couples don't even discuss retirement until it is upon them.

Keep in mind that if you retire at 65 and are fortunate enough to live past 90, your retirement savings will need to last more than 25 years. Additionally, health care costs and general inflation will impact your cost of living over the course of a quarter-century.

Make a habit of considering your financial future. Are those dollars you are spending at a mall or restaurant today better off saved or invested for tomorrow? If you purchase an item on credit, consider the true price you will pay including the interest.

Your fears are real. And, being able to trust someone like me doesn't come easily for most people.

After all, why should you trust me?

In the next few chapters, we'll take a closer look at the way I advise my clients and why I might be a great fit for helping you to save for your future.

I know the fear. I understand the emotions behind your eyes. Part of that fear is the client's expectation that the fact that they haven't saved enough will be confirmed. Will they be able to stay in their house? Can they remain independent? Will the next market crash do them in. Will they run out of money? Will they be able to cover health care costs?

The fear is real, but the solution is simple. My job is not about making sales—it's about changing lives.

Chapter 3

Insuring Your Income

What do I mean by insuring your income?

Well, let's think for a minute about our everyday lives. We insure or protect all of our assets, right?

We insure our lives, our health, our homes, our cars against liability for losses to others, and on and on. But what about our retirement income? Isn't insuring that asset as important as insuring our car against being liable for losses to others?

Of course it is. And that's why insuring your retirement income should be a no-brainer for you.

If you look at a Fixed Indexed Annuity in the simplest of terms, it is insurance for your retirement income. It means that you could have guaranteed lifetime income at a pre-determined amount for the remainder of your life and your spouse's life as well.

So, what is a Fixed Indexed Annuity?

Annuities are a source of guaranteed lifetime income that is back by someone. Historically, they have been backed by a variety of sources, but today's annuities are backed by insurance companies who are regulated by the Department of Insurance within each state.

This may surprise you, but nearly all Americans already have an annuity. It's called Social Security, and this retirement asset of yours is backed by the U.S. government. But even well before the genesis of Social Security, there were annuities in existence.

Did you know that George Washington, one of Americas wealthiest presidents, established annuities for his employees? He offered these retirement plans and backed them with his own money.

Why are Fixed Indexed Annuities important?

When Social Security was first created, life expectancies were 30 years less than they are now. Many people didn't even live long enough to start collecting Social Security. And, some only collected it for 5 years or so before they passed away.

There weren't the baby boomer numbers that we see today. People are living well into their 90's and there are significantly more people collecting Social Security income today.

An estimated 25 to 50 million people are living off of Social Security alone and barely getting by. So, when I started focusing on Fixed Index Annuities full time, I was utilizing a marketing program which generated SS maximization leads. People would see an ad online and then fill in their name to get more help.

I contacted many of these people and this was my first realization as to how dismal the retirement picture is for so many Americans. The majority of people who responded to my Social Security maximization advertisement were limited to their SS income and were looking for a miracle in hopes of squeezing more out of it. For most of them, this was the beginning and end of their retirement income options—no additional savings at all.

I met with them with the hopes that I could generate a strategy for them to provide an additional source of guaranteed lifetime income by adding Fixed Indexed Annuities to their portfolio.

Fixed Indexed Annuities are life changers. You probably have heard of them, but don't know of their ability to provide safe, secure and worry-free retirements. You may have doubts about them or you've heard negatives things.

Why do annuities sometimes get a bad rap?

It comes mostly from misinformation provided by brokers (see more on this in Chapter 5) and a general lack of knowledge about exactly how annuities work.

The truth is that Fixed Indexed Annuities, with a Guaranteed Lifetime Income Rider, provide guarantees that you just can't get in the risky stock market nor from a bank. They protect you from market downturns while providing guaranteed lifetime income, and a death benefit. Also, annuities can offer certain tax advantages.

The Guaranteed Lifetime Income Rider is an optional benefit that may be added to your annuity policy at issue for an annual fee of approximately 1%. This fee will vary from annuity to annuity and it is well worth it. Think of the fee as an insurance premium, which transfers the risk of you running out of retirement income to an insurance carrier. The Guaranteed Lifetime Income Rider can provide the owner with a Guaranteed Withdrawal Payment from his or her annuity that will last a lifetime—income that cannot be outlived.

The guaranteed lifetime income payments will continue until the death of the annuity owner, regardless of how long they live. If the owner dies there are two options:

1. The spouse can continue to receive the Guaranteed Withdrawal Payments for the rest of his/her lifetime.
2. The beneficiary can receive any remaining contract value.

How can an insurance company offer you these guarantees of downside market protection and guaranteed lifetime income?

Yes, of all the many wonderful features of Fixed Indexed Annuities (FIAs), the two most significant features are downside protection of our retirement assets from market volatility, along with guaranteed lifetime income. Even if you live to be 100 or more and your retirement savings becomes exhausted at age 85, or thereabouts, your income is guaranteed never to end until you do.

So, you'd think this would be music to the ears of most people when an agent describes these two comforting Fixed Indexed Annuity features. Instead, we quite often get a blank stare, as if to say, "How can those guys do that?"

To understand the answer to this question is to understand how insurance works. And yes, Fixed Indexed Annuities are retirement insurance policies. Many agents describe Fixed Indexed Annuities as the opposite of life insurance. Life insurance provides a hedge against not living long enough, resulting in a potential financial void. While Fixed Indexed Annuities provide a hedge against living too long and outliving your money in retirement.

Many people view insurance as a necessary evil, because its ongoing cost is a significant part of our living expenses. However, insurance is actually a brilliant financial concept. Think about what happened when a house burned down before the innovation of insurance. It was usually rebuilt through the help of loving neighbors, also known as labor pooling.

Today, the same concept works, but with the pooling of money instead of labor. When an insurance company has billions of our dollars in reserves, it's not a burden for them to indemnify one of their insured's when they suffer a total loss of their home, or are involved in a catastrophic auto accident, or outlive their retirement savings.

Furthermore, insurance companies invest the money we give them into long-term investments. This provides them with what they need in terms of profitability, enabling them to provide us with what we need depending on the type of insurance policy.

Most of us can't afford to assume the risk of losing our homes and writing a check for $300,000 to rebuild them if we've suffered a total loss from a fire or tornado. Most of us also can't afford to assume the loss with our autos if we total out another person's $80,000 auto or injure someone. In fact, because the loss (liability) effects other people, that's why it is a legal requirement for us to have auto insurance.

You are also transferring the risk of losing money in a down market. Commonly, people ages 55 and older don't want, or can't afford, to assume that risk on their own either. So an insurance company can assume it for them.

Recently, we went to a close friend's memorial service. One of his kids came up to me, shook my hand and said to me, "Thank you for taking care of my mom."

He had attended a meeting I'd had with his mother to review her finances after his father's death. I'd been able to help her create a solid, stable financial future years earlier. She could grieve in peace, comforted by knowing that she wouldn't be left with an income shortage in retirement.

Just like this situation, I help many of my clients protect their families financially. Similarly, I have created a retirement plan for myself and my wife that is safe, secure and worry-free, and I want to do the same for you.

Chapter 4

My Personal Thoughts on Retirement

Retirement in the United States has turned into an enormous challenge for middle income earners and I find it extremely disheartening.

Why am I so passionate about Fixed Indexed Annuities and helping people create a safe, secure and worry-free retirement?

As I mentioned in the last chapter, how can you beat guaranteed lifetime income? I mean, it is just that simple.

One of the best things that ever happened in our economy is when insurance companies got ahold of this in the 1920's and started being the backers, as apposed to individuals (like George Washington). A lot of agents talk about one of the first people that moved their money into annuities was Babe Ruth. In fact, it was what enabled him to survive the Great Depression.

Today, there are so many millions of middle income earners that don't have enough for retirement. It's common to see baby boomers with $50 to $200K saved (if that much), and they know it is not enough to retire on. This is where Fixed Indexed Annuities come in and help enormously.

Gambling with your money in a bank or brokerage account (if you live to be 90 or 95) is a formula for disaster. Insurance company backed Fixed Indexed Annuities can fill this gap. Banks or brokerage accounts aren't designed to assume retirement income shortfall risks like insurance companies can. Fixed Indexed Annuities are the only vehicle out there that provides retirement income shortfall coverage. You simply can't put your money in a bank or brokerage account and expect it to last that long.

Today, in a bank account, inflation is outpacing interest earnings alone. Of course, interest is taxable, unless the account is a tax deferred account, such as an IRA. With 2-3% inflation, there's no way you could put $200K in a bank account, drawdown $2K a month, and expect it to last until you're 95 years old.

Then, we have the growing concern of market volatility. And, market volatility is only going get much worse.

With a Fixed Indexed Annuity, you'll never run out of income. The insurance companies that assume this risk for you are regulated. You never see a life or annuity insurance company go out of business. You may find some that are not rated highly, but when that happens they typically will grow into a more favorable rating or become acquired by another carrier. This happens on occasion, but it's rare.

Often, people who are considering a Fixed Indexed Annuity are told or read that their annuity money isn't insured by the FDIC. That is true, but a Fixed Indexed Annuity is strongly protected. In fact, it already comes insured by the company who issued the annuity. And, if the insurance company fails, it has a secondary protection by the state guaranty association up to a maximum amount, as with the FDIC, determined by each state. State guaranty associations and the guaranty funds they manage provide a safety net for policyholders, ensuring that their annuity is protected and they will continue to receive their annuity benefits.

Because Fixed Indexed Annuities are insurance products, the insurance company who issues them and the insurance producer, like me, who sells them are regulated by the company's state Department of Insurance. The department is responsible to protect consumers and ensure the financial health of their state's insurance companies. The insurance industry is a strong part of the state's economy. Life and annuity insurance companies are the largest single source of bond finance for American business, holding 18% of all U.S. corporate bonds.

Then look at the downside protection. Fixed Indexed Annuities give you protection from market downturns and partial credit for the upside. If we enter into a bear market (when the price of an investment falls at least 20%) you won't lose sleep knowing that your account value is protected.

Personally, my wife and I have 10 annuities for various reasons. We are comfortable. I wouldn't recommend something to my clients that I don't believe in myself.

I just want to sit down with you and help you get to where we are—that same sort of comfort level. It is perplexing to me why so few people have an understanding about the features of Fixed Indexed Annuities and the comfort and security they offer. People put their money in banks and vulnerable security accounts without knowledge of the other options available to them.

This is a monumental problem in our country. Sure, you have to have money to put into annuities, it is not a magic fix, but it is amazing how this one type of retirement vehicle can change your life.

People just aren't getting educated enough with retirement planning. When it comes to finance, people plug their ears, close their eyes and run from education. Then, they pay the price for it when they get to their 60's.

This is why I'm so passionate about this. I would be that very same person if I hadn't ended up in this business.

I'll be open and honest here, as I stated in my introduction, until the age of 45, I didn't even know what a mutual fund was much less anything about Fixed Indexed Annuities. I was quite fortunate to get into this industry when I did. I want to help you create a plan so you don't have to gamble on getting lucky.

Chapter 5

But, My Broker Said…

By the time I first meet with a client, many of them have already been working with a broker for years. And, it's not that brokers are bad or have evil intentions. It's that their motive in guiding clients down a particular path is influenced by their own goals first, and their client's goals second.

Brokers are paid for assets under management. What does that mean? Typically, they are paid 1% annually for the management of your money. Let me give you an example, let's say you have $200,000 in a brokerage account. Your broker is earning $2,000 (1%) per year on your money. So, when you ask your broker, "What do you think about me moving $100,000 into an annuity?" What they are hearing is "What do you think about taking a cut in pay?"

The irony here is that you are their annuity! In this example, if you moved 50% of your money they would lose $1,000 per year in income. They want to discourage you from investing a part of your retirement assets into a safe vehicle with guarantees, but they want you to continue to provide them with annual income. I'm not saying that brokers are lying, but many of them are certainly misleading people, strategically, in order to retain their assets. This is very common.

There is an ongoing advertising campaign you may see on TV with, let's just call him, "Mr. I-Hate-Annuities." He ends the ad by saying, "Our structure is... When you do better, we do better." He fails to tell you that when you do worse, they still do better. Whatever that 1% is.

So, they will always advise you not to transfer your money into any other type of investment (annuity, investment property, etc.) vehicle. On the flip side, I don't have the same motive. My job is to make sure that you and your family are provided for, for the rest of your life.

Another thing I've seen brokers do is refer to their systematic withdrawal plans as annuities. Don't be fooled. Ask them what their plan is for guaranteed lifetime income, no matter how long you live. If they don't have an answer, then they are just using annuity as a word to retain your assets. Remember, Fixed Indexed Annuities are insurance policy products, not an investment vehicle. Brokers are in the business to maintain income annually on your assets. Fixed Indexed Annuities don't pay out that way.

How do I get paid? I get an upfront commission when the Fixed Indexed Annuity policy is issued. And, it's paid out of the insurance companies reserves, not by my client. You'll never see any management fees debited from your account. I never make another penny after the upfront commission once the annuity is issued.

I recently met with some clients who have four Fixed Indexed Annuities I've written for them. They asked me why there was so much confusion and misinformation about Fixed Indexed Annuities. This is a common question I hear all the time. When I explained to them that so much of it comes out of brokerage firms, he stated, "That should be illegal."

I have to say that I agree.

As regulated as the financial industry is, there is nothing to stop a broker from making certain comments to deter the investor from making a change. When a Fixed Indexed Annuity strategy for market protection and guaranteed lifetime income is presented to them for a second opinion, they'll say something like "This concerns me." A response like that may plant seeds of doubt in your mind.

I battle this all the time.

If a broker says, "Why would you want to tie your money up in an annuity?" I counter that with, "Why would you want to risk running out of money during retirement?"

So, what is meant by "tied up" anyway? Annuities, just like permanent life insurance policies (such as whole life or universal life), have surrender periods. When you move money into an annuity, a portion of it is held by the insurance carrier for a period of 6-16 years usually, with a certain amount of liquidity, usually 10%.

Why is this? The way insurance companies make money is by investing our money into long term investments. So they are saying, "If you provide us with what we need, we will in turn, provide you with what you need." Which is, by the way, downside protection and guaranteed lifetime income.

Recently, I showed an income report to an existing client. I wanted to show her what income she could expect each year throughout her retirement. She was ecstatic. When she saw her retirement report she said, "I'm scheduling a cruise!"

It is this type of comment from my clients that drives me.

The current turmoil of the stock market may be even more unsettling for investors with just a few years to go until retirement. Avoiding wrong moves amid the turmoil could be even more critical.

The stock market is inherently risky. You can double your money if you guess right or lose half of it if you guess wrong. A lot can happen in a short period of time.

In 2008, some people saw as much as a 50% loss. A recent correction saw the Dow Jones industrial average lose 10% of its value. This may feel like a calamity if your tolerance for risk has diminished and you are watching your retirement savings shrink. A loss of 10% in the first 5 years of retirement can shorten a portfolio's life by 10 to 15 years.

While investors should avoid panicking over short-term movements in the value of their long-term investments, the recent volatility ought to serve as a wake-up call to re-examine risk and stress-test your portfolio against the possibility of further declines. If the thought of a certain percentage drop in your portfolio makes you break out in a cold sweat, it's time to dial down the risk.

This is what brokers don't want you to know and what I want to help you solve, with Fixed Indexed Annuities.

Chapter 6

Conventional Investments

Let's take a moment to discuss other types of investments for your retirement.

Banks

Investing money in savings and CD's, and taking subsequent systematic withdrawals during retirement will likely result in two things.

1. With interest rates as low as they are now, and have been for years, it is highly unlikely your growth will outpace inflation. Plus, your growth is taxable (unless it is in a tax deferred account) on an annual basis.
2. Although eliminating market volatility will make your annual growth, minus annual withdrawal numbers, much

more predictable, what is still unpredictable is how long you will live, at least in most cases.

Fixed Indexed Annuities compared to Variable Annuities:

Up until now, I've mentioned the safety and security of Fixed Indexed Annuities numerous times. Fixed Indexed Annuities are not to be confused with Variable Annuities. I want to explain how the growth of your principal differs with each one. When you transfer your retirement savings from a brokerage account into a Variable Annuity, you are essentially moving your money from one account exposed to market volatility to another account exposed to market volatility.

Variable Annuities are made up of mutual funds that are designed especially for the Variable Annuity. These funds are referred to sub-accounts. But, once again, they are essentially mutual funds within the Variable Annuity subject to just as much market volatility as the brokerage account was prior to the transfer.

If you have gotten to the age where your tolerance for risk is diminishing, a Variable Annuity may not make sense for you.

A Fixed Indexed Annuity credits your principal with a portion of the market upside, but with 0% of the market downside. That is one of two features that make a Fixed Indexed Annuity an insurance product versus a Variable Annuity, which is a security product.

Because your retirement assets are invested in mutual funds within the Variable Annuity, they need to be managed by a fund manager. You are paying an annual fee for those management services.

With a Fixed Indexed Annuity, there are no management services required, so there are no management fees. The management fees for sub-accounts within a Variable Annuity are very high—2 to 4% on top of the potential of losses due to market downturns.

I don't offer Variable Annuities and I don't recommend them. You can develop a very successful retirement income plan without taking these kinds of risks.

One additional thought on Fixed Indexed Annuities I would like to pass along. Never buy a proprietary Fixed Indexed Annuity product. There are two types of insurance agents that offer annuities—captive and independent.

Let me explain these briefly.

Captive:

Captive agents represent one company and are contractually bound to represent their products only. This business model removes the company from competition at the agent level. When they are removed from competition, the carrier has no incentive to offer the most consumer friendly annuity products.

Why should they give away more, when they don't have to? And, usually, the agent doesn't even realize that their company's product(s) are potentially inferior to the consumer as opposed to other companies' products that are subject to a tremendous amount of competition from 30-40 other companies.

Independent:

As I mentioned in my introduction, I started in the insurance and financial services business in 1998, when I was 45 years old.

I represented one company for 14 years with a captive contract, so I know how they work.

I sold my agency and book of business in 2011 and went independent. I wanted more retirement options for my clients. Because I was captive for so many years, when I first entered the independent distribution channel, I knew I would have more (and better) options for my clients, but I didn't realize how much better.

Let's just say, carriers who offer annuity products in the independent channel fall all over themselves developing consumer friendly products that beat the competition. Then, another annuity company releases an annuity product that is superior to the others. The never ending research I'm committed to is challenging, but it's still fun to watch. I love presenting better and better options for my clients.

The stock market is up, the stock market is down, day after day and it is completely unpredictable. Stress among many people concerned about their financial stability in retirement is very high. If you have experienced recent gains in your retirement accounts, but are worried about what's next, answer these questions to determine if the "Retirement Gambling" system is still for you at this stage of your life.

1. Do you find yourself thinking about ways to still achieve growth of your retirement nest egg, but want to protect it at the same time?

2. Are you becoming more and more concerned each year with the volatility of the U.S. and world economy?

3. Do you wonder if you'll have enough income during retirement?

4. If there is a market crash or two during your retirement, do you worry about running out of money?
5. Do you wonder if you could outlive your retirement nest egg if you lived 20 or more years into retirement?

If you share some or all of these feelings, consider a simple and guaranteed approach to retirement planning instead.

With a Fixed Indexed Annuity, when these markets move up, your account is credited. When the market lowers itself, you do not participate. Your account can only increase and never decrease. Here's the catch, your funds are not invested in these indexes, they are used simply to calculate what your account value is credited with.

There are numerous companies and a myriad of products available, so make certain your choice matches with your goals. Think "Gain or Retain" for your important retirement dollars and remove all risk.

In the past few years, a perfect storm has been slowly developing, a storm that will have a negative effect on retirement planning. Since the financial downslide America faced in 2007, general interest rates have declined to historic lows, resulting in a very low interest rate offered by US Treasuries, which are the financial backbone for investment used by insurance companies. Since US Treasuries provide a fully guaranteed asset, many companies have a large percentage of their assets in this category.

Instead of personally managing your retirement funds or allowing a financial planner or stockbroker to manage them, move your funds to an insurance company. An insurance company will issue you a Fixed Indexed Annuity based on an underlying guarantee. That guarantee is simple: your funds will never lose value and will never be exposed to market risk. The removal of the possibility of losses provides a guaranteed base on which future growth will be added.

Many consumers are frightened and confused about what road to take with their retirement assets given current, and future, market conditions. You are not alone. Most people in the U.S. have those same feelings.

Chapter 7

Top 10 Retirement Planning Excuses

Have you been putting off planning for your retirement? Once again, you're not alone. I've put together the Top 10 Retirement Planning Excuses list along with some advice.

Let's count them down…

10. "I'm too busy."

Stop procrastinating. Retirement may be for dinosaurs, like me, but you will be one before you know it.

9. "It's too soon."

It's NEVER too soon. The sooner you start planning, the better chance you stand of having the kind of retirement you desire.

8. "It's too late."

Get disciplined and buckle down. Even if you're already retired, it's important to consider how you're receiving income and how long it will last.

7. "I don't need to."

Seriously! If you're arbitrarily giving monthly to a retirement savings account and hoping for the best, you will be in for an unpleasant surprise someday.

6. "I don't have enough money to get started."

Join the club! Starting small is better than not starting at all. And if you plan well, you'll eventually have more to work with.

5. "My finances are a disorganized."

I can help. We can look together at your current financial picture and develop a plan to turn your "retirement disorganization" into an "organized plan." You will feel relief that you are on a trajectory that you understand and feel good about.

4. "The Government will take care of me."

Stop kidding yourself? If you're planning to retire on Social Security alone, I would advise you to create a back-up plan at the very least.

3. "Between my savings and my 401(k), I'll be fine."

Savings plans are different from income plans. Saving for retirement without an income distribution plan is a mistake. Have you considered inflation? Taxes? If you live to 100, will your money last?

2. "I don't want to think about it."

This one actually makes me a little angry. Think about it now or you will be thinking about it a lot more in the future, like at 2:00 a.m.

And the number one #1 retirement planning excuse is…

1. "I don't know how."

There's no such thing as an innate ability to master retirement planning. I totally get it. If you're better at History and English than you are at Math and Finance, you're not alone. But, make a serious commitment to learning, and find a professional who can help you.

Plus, that's what I'm here for. Take advantage of the material I've offered in this book and schedule an appointment with me in the near future. I'd love to see what I can do to help you avoid financial problems in your retirement years.

Chapter 8

The Conclusion

Now that I've explained my retirement planning thoughts and reasoning to you. Now that I've shared how and why I found my way into retirement planning. Now that I've done my best to convince you of the absolute necessity of investing in a Fixed Indexed Annuity. I want to take a moment to share a little more with you about my friends Steve and Marcia.

Remember when I mentioned earlier in the book about a friend who had passed away and how her son approached me after his father's memorial service to thank me?

Well, my wife, Becky, and I first met Steve and Marcia on November 26, 2006. We had just moved from Elizabeth, Colorado to Monument, Colorado after building a spec home in Monument. The housing market collapsed shortly afterwards and we had to move into the spec home we thought was going to be for someone else.

God had a different plan for us. Our current home would be easier to sell, so we put it on the market and moved into the spec home.

We met them that Sunday at a non-denominational church, about two miles from the Monument home we had reluctantly just moved into. After church, they invited us out to lunch. God blessed Becky and I as we subsequently became lifelong friends with Steve and Marcia. Since that first meal, we've had dozens of meals together, taken day trips together, weekend trips together, and last summer, we spent 19 days together on a European vacation.

In early 2014, Steve called me and asked if I would show Marcia and him how Fixed Indexed Annuities worked. Of course, I did. Soon after, they rolled a significant portion of his in-service 401(k) money into one.

Subsequently, my advice to them was to continue to contribute to Steve's 401(k) to take advantage of the matching contribution from his employer, along with potential growth. Approximately once per year, at strategic points of market growth, we would roll more into new annuities in order to protect that growth and add to their future retirement income. We did this three times after the initial transaction in early 2014.

In 2015, they chose to start a $250,000 life insurance policy. They had recently moved and thought it would be wise to have a policy to cover their mortgage.

Recently, in 2019, my good friend Steve went home to be with the Lord. He was only 64 years old. His employer allowed him to work at home on Fridays. At some point during the day, he laid down to take a nap, and passed away in his sleep. We were all stunned.

Recently, I met with Marcia to review their finances. She had a remaining mortgage on her house and a loan on a new car they recently purchased. Marcia is self-employed and would like to continue to work, but, at 64, how much longer, and how often, is undetermined.

I advised Marcia to pay off those debts with the life insurance death benefit. Steve was the contract holder of the four annuities, because the money originated as his 401(k) money and was rolled into IRA money within the annuities. Marcia was the primary beneficiary with all four annuities and Steve's life policy. I told her if she continued the annuity contracts in her name, her income, if taken now on all four annuities, would more than cover her income needs going forward, guaranteed for life, with no debt because of the life insurance.

This was why her son thanked me at the memorial service. This is how I took care of his mom. This is what gratifies me as I continue to do this for a living.

I help people create their retirement income futures that are safe, secure and worry-free, without the fears of being broke or having to work into their 70's and 80's.

I can do something similar for you.

Just prior to writing this portion of the book, my wife and I were discussing Marcia's life, going forward without Steve. I said, "They trusted me. I wish more people would trust me this way." We both cried and held each other—tears for the loss of Steve and tears resulting from the thought of God using me to help bless Marcia's financial future.

Thank you for reading this book. I look forward to hearing from you in the near future.

About the Author

Mike and his wife Becky enjoy the life most people dream about. Through hard work, good planning, and the proper investment strategy, they have the peace of mind that comes with knowing their income is guaranteed for life. Mike now works, not because he has to, but because he loves helping people reach their retirement dream and protect the assets they've worked so hard to accumulate.

Mike's experience in life and financial services gives him a unique perspective. You'll sense his desire to help from your first conversation. Talking with Mike is like sharing coffee with a good friend. Making sure you understand and are comfortable taking the next step is paramount to how he cares for his clients. That's one reason he named his company Paramount Financial Resources.

When he's not working with clients, Mike enjoys vacationing with Becky, and spending time with their two daughters and sons-in-law, along with their four grandchildren. Mike also enjoys baseball, driving in the mountains, and is an active member of First Baptist Church of Black Forest in Colorado Springs.

Made in the USA
Monee, IL
04 November 2026

67387303R00026